THE QUOTABLE FELINE

THE
QUOTABLE
FELINE

JIM DRATFIELD

AND

PAUL COUGHLIN

PETOGRAPHY, INC.

ALFRED A. KNOPF NEW YORK 1996

A NOTE ON THE TYPE

This book is set in a typeface called Bulmer. This distinguished letter is a replica of a type long famous in the history of English printing and was designed and cut by William Martin about 1790 for William Bulmer of the Shakespeare Press. In design, it is all but a modern face, with vertical stress, sharp differentiation between the thick and thin strokes, and nearly flat serifs. The decorative italic shows the influence of Baskerville, as Martin was a pupil of John Baskerville's.

Separations and printing by Hull Printing,
Meriden, Connecticut

Binding by Horowitz Rae,
Fairfield, New Jersey

Book design by Carol Devine Carson

To Lee Dratfield, Lena Esposito, and Sue Shaw for their devotion and unique ability
to live all of their nine lives to the fullest.

J . D .

To all friends human and animal—Walnut, Jerry, Connie, and Sabina

P . C .

A C K N O W L E D G M E N T S

A heartfelt thank you to our agent, Susan Golomb, for providing inspiration; to Carol Carson for her impeccable sense of design; to Katherine Hourigan for her insight and encouragement; and to Andy Hughes for his wizardry and inexhaustible energy.

We acknowledge with gratitude the kind help of Phyllis Levy, Roberta Altman, Dr. Donald Williams, Marti Andersen, and the indispensable Rose Wagner. A special thank you to Judy Yee, Robert Gordon, Jane Gordon, Terry W. Sanders, and the William Secord Gallery. A round of applause goes to Rea, Zeke, Shalom, Ben, Tom, David, and Josh—and thank you to all the cats who stayed still long enough to be photographed.

THE QUOTABLE FELINE

Cats are intended to teach us that not

everything in nature has a function.

———————

G a r r i s o n K e i l l o r

Between two evils, I always

pick the one I never tried before.

———

Klondike Annie,
as played by Mae West

The smallest feline is a masterpiece.

———

Leonardo da Vinci

I purr, therefore I am.

———————

A n o n y m o u s

Thanks to the soothing, the bliss,...

we seemed to understand each other.

We had crossed our species' boundaries

and had found the common center in

each other, where all creatures rest.

———

Elizabeth Marshall Thomas

The cat of the slums and alleys,

starved, outcast, harried,...still displays

the self-reliant watchfulness which man has

never taught it to lay aside.

S a k i

A friend is, as it were, a second self.

———

Cicero

Who can believe that there is no soul

behind those luminous eyes!

———

Théophile Gautier

Most cats, when they are Out want to be In,

and vice versa, and often simultaneously.

———

Louis J. Camuti, D.V.M.

One meets the cat in nearly all forms of art...

Curiously enough she is not a conspicuous

figure in Roman or Greek art.

———

Carl Van Vechten

One cat just leads to another.

———————

E r n e s t   H e m i n g w a y

The phrase "domestic cat" is an oxymoron.

———

G e o r g e   F .   W i l l

A pharaoh's profile, a Krishna's grace,

tail like a question mark.

———

L o u i s   M a c N e i c e

By associating with the cat,

one only risks becoming richer.

―――――

C o l e t t e

Intelligence in the cat is underrated.

———

Louis Wain

And let me touch those curving claws

of yellow ivory, and grasp the tail that

like a monstrous asp coils round

your heavy velvet paws.

———

O s c a r   W i l d e

I love cats because I enjoy my home;

and little by little,

they become its visible soul.

———

Jean Cocteau

Imitation is the sincerest of flattery.

———

Charles Caleb Colton

Dogs come when they're called; cats take a

message and get back to you.

———

M a r y   B l y

The wildcat is the "real" cat,

the soul of the domestic cat; unknowable

to human beings, he yet exists inside our

household pets, who have long ago seduced

us with their seemingly civilized ways.

———

Joyce Carol Oates

Way down deep, we're all motivated by

the same urges. Cats have

the courage to live by them.

———

Jim Davis

Her function is to sit and

be admired.

———————

Georgina Strickland Gates

I believe cats to be spirits come to earth. A cat, I am sure, could walk on a cloud without coming through.

———

Jules Verne

Of all animals, the cat alone attains to the

contemplative life. He regards the wheel

of existence from without,

like the Buddha.

A n d r e w   L a n g

Thou art the Great Cat, the avenger of the

gods, and the judge of words, and the

president of the sovereign chiefs and the governor

of the holy Circle; thou art indeed...

the Great Cat.

———

*Inscription on the
royal tombs at Thebes*

There is no more intrepid explorer

than a kitten.

———

Jules Champfleury

If a fish is the movement of water

embodied, given shape, then a cat

is a diagram and pattern

of subtle air.

———

Doris Lessing

It is in the nature of cats to do a certain

amount of unescorted roaming.

———

A d l a i   S t e v e n s o n

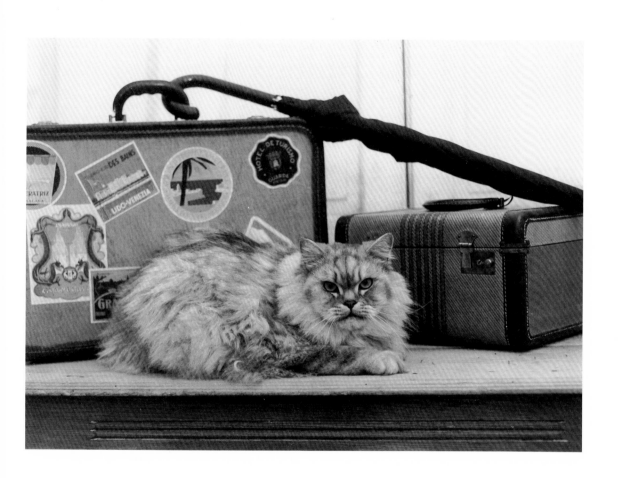

And gaze into your gazing eyes,

And wonder in a demi-dream

What mystery it is that lies

Behind those slits that glare and gleam...

———

Lytton Strachey

He possessed nothing in the world except

a cat, which he carried in his bosom,

frequently caressing it, as his sole companion.

———

Jacobus Diaconus

What is the victory of a cat on a hot tin roof?...

Just staying on it, I guess,

as long as she can.

———

Tennessee Williams

A cat has absolute emotional honesty:

human beings, for one reason or another,

may hide their feelings,

but a cat does not.

———

Ernest Hemingway

One of the oldest human needs is having

someone to wonder where you are when

you don't come home at night.

Margaret Mead

The greater cats with golden eyes

Stare out between the bars.

Deserts are there, and different skies,

And night with different stars.

Vita Sackville-West

Balanchine has trained his cat to perform

brilliant *jetés* and *tours en l'air*;

he says that at last he has a body worth

choreographing for.

———

Bernard   Taper

Cats don't belong to people.

They belong to places.

———

Wright Morris

As anyone who has ever been around a cat

for any length of time well knows,

cats have enormous patience with the

limitations of the human mind.

———

Cleveland Amory

If a cat did not put a firm paw down

now and then, how could his human

remain possessed?

———

Winifred Carriere

Like those great sphinxes lounging through

eternity in noble attitudes upon the

desert sand, they gaze incuriously

at nothing, calm and wise.

———

C h a r l e s   B a u d e l a i r e

Cats, no less liquid than their shadows,

Offer no angles to the wind.

They slip, diminished, neat, through loopholes

Less than themselves.

———

A . S . J .   T e s s i m o n d

I soon realized the name Pouncer in no way

did justice to her aerial skills.

By the end of the first day

I had amended her name to Kamikaze.

———

C l e v e l a n d   A m o r y

A cat pours his body on the floor like water.

It is restful just to see him.

———

William Lyon Phelps

Again I must remind you that

a Dog's a Dog—a CAT'S a CAT.

_T . S . E l i o t_

INDEX

A NOTE ABOUT THE AUTHORS

JIM DRATFIELD

Originally from Princeton, New Jersey, Jim Dratfield spent fourteen years as an actor on Broadway and on television, most notably in the recurring role of Bud Keiser on the series *St. Elsewhere*. He created O. Drat! Productions and produced Lanford Wilson's *Fifth of July* on the West Coast. His love of animals and photography led to his co-creation of Petography, Inc., of which he is Creative Director. He is the coauthor with Paul Coughlin of *The Quotable Canine*.

PAUL COUGHLIN

Paul Coughlin has been fascinated by photography for as long as he can remember. His images are featured on book jackets, greeting cards, calendars, and posters. Paul prefers sepia-toned black-and-white photography for its distinctive gentle other-era quality. He lives in Greenwich Village.

Petography, Inc., is devoted to fine art photography of pets and their people.
For further information on their services and a catalogue of items write:

Petography, Inc.
P.O. Box 20244
Columbus Circle Station
New York, NY 10023